In Which She Takes Multiple Lovers
and other poems

by Liana DeMasi

Copyright © 2021 Liana DeMasi. All rights reserved.

The characters and events portrayed in this book are fictitious. Any similarity to real persons, living or dead, is coincidental and not intended by the author.

No part of this book may be reproduced, or stored in a retrieval system, or transmitted in any form or by any means, electronic, mechanical, photocopying, recording, or otherwise, without express written permission of the publisher.

ISBN: 978-1-954657-00-7

Cover design by: Cass Reeder
Library of Congress Control Number: 2018675309
Printed in the United States of America

For every lover.

On History

I have tried to learn you. Your skin, your insides, the curve of your tongue, the way the moon follows you home. I have studied you in excess. The way the cobblestones seem to repurpose themselves beneath your feet. The way words sit in the back of my throat—or don't. The way that every time I attempt to write of you, I accuse myself of perjury. My knuckles bleed, rigor mortis around the ink pen as I tirelessly attempt a useless task.

But then the room is made empty by your absence. The mirrors shatter, and I am left with notebooks, a history of a person I do not know.

In Which She Reclaims Her Name

My parent's friends would always look at me and say:

"You're going to be trouble when you get older."

Prophetic and abusive, a deciding factor.

An image painted of full dance cards and male desire, my father up late on the couch, waiting for my arrival.

I didn't want to be trouble. I wanted to be a veterinarian, a teacher, an astronaut.

Some of the first words I remember hearing were:

"You're quite something,"

By which they meant my face was at the appropriate level of attractive at 10-years-old in order to convince me my worth would be measured in substances too small to fit in tablespoons, like beauty and one's ability to keep underfoot and undetected. Somewhere in there was:

"I love you,"

But the order doesn't matter much. The wires were crossed anyway.

I wish I had been told I was

    kind,
        capable,

intelligent, overflowing with anything other than premature sexuality.

Now I don't know how to write of much else: acts of sex and the world on fire.

I wonder if it's because I'm trying to burn a bridge someone else built for me.

I search for eyes in the night, a pair I might plead to, but I am met with empty glances, reminders I am alone.

And it is true. Sometimes, I am not pretty. The notes left are not for me.

Sometimes, I am trouble.

I work to defy you. A siren in the water, my call being only of existence, a vision inscribed by Adam, his kin. You will come un-beckoned and drown in tears of resistance. In the blood of martyrs.

I will spread my legs, welcoming only to the space they wish to take up. I will caress my own thighs, finger scar tissue on public transport. I will offend you in my aversion to you.

Silence will spit in the mouth of rage. The former will be neglected, the latter, critiqued. But they will rarely be seen as lovers.

The male-gaze is vulture-like, a predator atop a

house. Fire will fall from my mouth like peach juice, refreshing in its clarity, in its nostalgic yearning for an alternate future. It will be a rebirth, the erosion of a monolith.

The ones you labeled trouble will see smoke and rise valiantly to the occasion, victory cries against malice. Quite troublesome the revolution will be.

Quite troublesome indeed.

In Which Time Is Silence

The family heirloom is a pocket watch, so that you might feel the lack of time as a generational affliction, covered in gold.

Time is measured in silence.

Three years can pass beneath a willow tree that's immersed in a love affair with the wind. By the time you feel the urge to check the time, only five minutes will have passed.

I want to lie with you in the river, but it will have useless effects. Neither of us remember tranquility, adverse we are to strolling a stone's throw to recall it. Instead, we choose the regularity of four walls and a routine, pocket watches in their rightful places. By the time we feel the urge to check, it will have been years.

Is being conversational an affliction?

There is no "or" in this world.

I want for you to baptize me. But leave God at home. I want for you to hold me beneath the water. Must I cleanse for rebirth?

Time is tangible, loose change in a pocket.

The family heirlooms are a pocket watch and a Bible. My sisters and I choose nudity. The Bible burns in my right hand, and I flip through with an eagerness that only comes when one is hopeful for something they will not find. My thumb grazes the pocket watch. It has been an eternity.

A lover and I make it down by the river. She asks to be baptized, but I tell her I can't. I mustn't. Seconds turn to minutes turn to hours. The baptized have drowned.

In Which Eve Spoke

Adam landed in the garden, opened his eyes, and assumed he grew it.

In the first case of heresy (hearsay), Adam created Eve and, simultaneously, a God Complex.

Discovering his tongue, Adam began to misuse it.

"You have big, beautiful eyes. I love when they look up at me."
"Your hair. Keep it long, gives me something to pull on."
"I love how thick your thighs are."

    And then later,

"Your thighs are too thick."
"Don't you think you should shave?"
"I don't understand why you're not more comfortable."
"I would go down on you if your vagina didn't look like that."
"I love your hips. Something to grab on to."
"Those lips."
    "Those lips."
        "Those lips."
            "Those lips."

Eve, who was perplexed by her alleged creation from Adam's rib, listened to the man in awe. Where had he gained such an understanding of the world, of the female body, having been on Earth only briefly without her?

Where had he gained such an understanding of the world, of the female body, being only a cis man?

Days later, grappling with the apparent downfall of humanity through her consumption of an apple, Eve spoke:

My kin will have weighted tongues. There will come a day when the mouths you imprison will untie themselves and rise from the depths you have placed them in. Their "no," will reduce the air in your lungs to nothing. Then, in brevity, you will be equals. Your kin will rely on the recitation of the words "all men" like it might   absolve them. But the words will become more selective than cancer, until they, perhaps not until death, realize they themselves were the disease. It is me you will look up at.

My hair will be long, and short, and long again. It will be brown, red, pink, black. It will be punished, cut off, shaved, ripped out, and otherwise become another thing that is not mine. Eventually, I will dye it blue and cut it short, feigning for a moment that it constitutes bodily autonomy.

You will forsake, destroy, and profit upon the body that these thighs uphold, creating a dichotomy between body and mind so influential, that it will take me years to understand that I can love myself without your permission.

I want to braid it. I want to pull at it out of boredom. You have no idea my relationship with a razor. *Put your arms above your heads, my dears. Allow the hair to get some air. Wear shorts and yank. Go full bush. Let your hair down.*

To be comfortable is a privilege that you have already taken from me.

I need you to go down on me in the same way the world needs more cis-white, heterosexual men believing they have power simply because they were born.

My hips are not metal bars used for balance. I am not your lighthouse. What you will learn when these hips fill up a seat at the table.

And those lips. I will tell you about those lips. The words that sit on the tongue they protect will burn cities, raise mountains, and, at the least, put you in your place. Those lips will be good for bedtime kisses and sexual deviance. I will apologize for neither, though you will force my hand every time. They will beg for strawberries and receive semen. They will still say thank you because they will be taught to remain grateful to be considered at all. They will recite unpublished poetry until blood pours down chins. These lips will be burned last when I go. Or else, preserved. A National Treasure.

In Which The World is Made

At the base of Mt. Vesuvius, bodies are frozen in love and despair. There is beauty found in death - innately - as declared by man. They say we are at war with one another. But to classify something as war is to hold it dichotomous to peace. I see no evidence of that.

The Leviathan sits thick with purpose.

Mother gives me a pillow and tells me to close my eyes, to meditate and manifest upon the world I seek to exist in. But the pillow seems too soft and delicate for matters such as these. I am reminded the world falls each day for much less.

I love to whisper, but what violence lies in silence.

I meditate on a world where women came home late for dinner with stained collars, burdened by unrecognized freedom. But the image is blurry with falsity. Because it may be more honest to admit that our poise, patience, and kindness are just as much products of our oppression as our rage.

In this world, our formidable attractions are not fortresses and old army vessels. But I cannot, no matter how hard I shut my eyes, imagine what might take their places.

A woman's anger was slow drip coffee, hidden notes in the morning paper. You cannot convince me no tears were shed in writing *A Room of One's Own*.

In Paris, I sat with Wilde for a while. I read notes left at his grave, rather invasively. They were not for me. I found Colette's — finally, after searching. It stood empty.

Wilde was rightfully revered, but at the intersection of queerness and womanhood, therein lies a ditch. We forgot each other before we had the chance to start.

What if they couldn't quote *De Profundis*? What if they're leaving notes for a dead man because they know somewhere deep-seated in death is unimaginable beauty and implacable longing, the fullness of a life eclipsed.

I left Colette a note, dressing empty grass. We will be weeping for an eternity for Baldwin, Lorde, Parker. You will begin to consider the ineptitude of your own grief.

We live amongst Deniers, those with upturned noses at the written word. The world has been drawn a Liar. And in this, we have been set up for failure, eyes always peeled for Judas. How many of us identify with Lucifer, perhaps just the first of us gravely misunderstood and cast aside.

At least he is the ruler of something.

In this world I meditate upon, history is different. There are many portraits of women in purple, their hands atop a walking staff. The lines in history books telling stories of army generals turn into queer erotica. Galileo was bisexual. Aphrodite was trans.

Charles Darwin was a pseudonym. Sisyphus was a woman. Jesus and their many counterparts was non-binary, was queer, was Black, was POC, was fat—was any of us who must carry the burden of a boulder up the mountain, being that the boulder is marginalization and being that the mountain was built while too many men were reciting the Lord's Prayer in vain.

There remains poetry at all their graves, well-read followers weeping at their feet.

On Love and Queerness

Time was spent telling the wrong people I loved them. Perhaps, once, I did. It is more likely, though, that I longed to. Queer was some victory proclamation that I couldn't pronounce.

Freedom was for someone else. Queer meant peculiar; gay meant happy, and I tried so hard not to be one, that I was neither.

That first love might kill you, but queer love is liberation. There are so many stories to tell.

I am grateful for everyday that I live in the aftermath, the feathers risen from dust, bursting with the color that sits in the mortar and pestle of oppression and strength.

The voices of my fore-queers ring loudly in my soul. For I am becoming each day, made possible by their having navigated that queer meant peculiarly happy, despite the odds.

**For my queer family who are unable to live openly in this world, we will continue to work tirelessly to liberate our people, to create a world that may not understand, but at best, makes room.

***For my fallen queer family. Thank you for existing, even in brevity. How shameful that the world was so afraid of your light, your beauty. Nothing is in vain. For Fallen Black Trans Women especially, I stand with you in solidarity, education, and advocacy. You are the pinnacle of power and beauty. May you rest in both.

In Which She Tries Faulkner

Time wallowed in the river; the night air released the day's stronghold, your voice like gravel in my ear.

I am wanted on a voyage. But I cannot bear to go.

The bookseller wore a hat that suited him. I wanted to know him because I wanted to know anyone. Instead, I overpaid him for a French-translated copy of *As I Lay Dying*. I wished for it to speak to me.

My body slack against concrete, my feet in the Rhône. You whispered false prophecies in my ear from across the Atlantic.

Wine tainted my lips and clarified my thoughts. A man asked me what I was writing. I lied and told him love letters. In a thick French accent, he told me love was universal. What I mean to say is, so many of us are empty.

How could I write a book of poetry without writing of you? I never thought you hung the moon, however convinced I was it followed you home. I wanted you to quote, *It's a Wonderful Life*, my pointer finger hanging in the air. Instead, you took my finger in your mouth, and I filled in the blanks myself.

I wanted to be the map of France on your wall. I wanted to hang on your tongue like Bordeaux did. I wanted you to consider me, wine in a glass. But eventually I became a stranger in your bed, a stale smell on fingers.

Are you part of my birth, or part of my death? Or else, do you dwell with me in the fields between?

I am wanted on a voyage. But I cannot bear to go.

In Which ~~Queer~~ Sex is An Abomination

My pussy pulsates in the mouth of my lover. My clitoris is a Minotaur, a thing demonized yet prophetic, and I feel I might be able to count its nerve endings against her taste buds. We whisper thank you in unison because, however in brevity, the shame hanging in the air is masked by sex and pre-cum.

I am thirstier than I've ever been.

I want to worship her body, but what I mean to say is, I want to appreciate it with a ferocity that attempts to heal it. But what I mean to say is, I want to lie with her in distraction. For the power of a person will always be limited by the very fact of their existence.

I am not a goddess of any element. My skin is not elastic, and I will one day be ash. But the moments in which our bodies root in ancestry while becoming boundless, two souls indeterminable from one another, I can count the teeth in her mouth with my womanhood, and I am victim to nothing but my own weakness.

To be thirsty and quenched at once.

I promise there is reproduction here. Every time in the arch of a back and the bite of a lip and the shudder of a body wracked with pleasure. I see colors and shapes when I close my eyes, a slack line tying my feet to a tree. I am nature, a Minotaur atop a hill. I will find pride in my demonization, as you light fires beneath my feet.

I am the color of rage, the blue hue of warmth in the pit. My legs part to reveal the sea, men-less and beckoning.

In Which She Submerges Herself

An ex-girlfriend once shaved her head.

"Are you angry?"
"Do you like it?"

Soft reminders that our existence begins and ends with asking permission.

"I don't feel sexy."

A line derived in the idea that our appeal is only physical.

We eat approval first and food second, upbringings of unprocessed food and diction. At birth, we are assigned names we will later denounce, and given tools in which to determine how others see themselves. We are told not to worry about the pain of a scalpel, for Evolution has made us strong, resilient, and self-hating.

If you go deep enough you'll see the words of your predecessors.

"Are you angry?"
"Do you like it?"

Anger is often possessive, pronounced, inarticulate. But Athena was rarely questioned, her kin rightfully triumphed. Here, in the Theory of Anger Over the Presentation of a Lover, anger is misplaced, in that it is placed at all. I am here for your soul. It is that which I aim to kiss as the Sunday Morning Light comes on you. Am I angry? Maybe envious. I can't fathom the thought.

We were born on the diving board.

Some days it's back down the ladder; other days it's a free-fall of yielding to gravity. As you tumble, you think: this is the day I'll do what they call succumbing, what they call drowning. As your body meets water you're reminded of your beginnings.

To be submerged and to not feel panicked. To be touched and to not feel violated.

What Love Language is this? There is rebirth here, and for the first time in a while you think the Universe understands you. You understand you are of Her, that she is of You.

She means to wash you, absolve you. Turn the words written on your body to nothing but smudged reminders of Life Before.

Slut.

Dyke.

Fat.

Lacking in potential.

Hairy.

Try-hard.

Too loud.

Not funny.

Ugly crier.

Here we weep. Deep down in this water, we scream, but nothing fills our lungs because this water understands we need rest. This water understands we are ashamed of ourselves because we were born on third base with shackles around our ankles, and that made it hard to watch as Others ran passed us, writing declarations on our skins.

We emerge, refreshed with our new skin. Our First Skin. The sun feels strong because it is hitting that spot for the first time. It's crawling into you, and you allow it. This is what your mother meant by Radiating.

"Are you angry?"
"Do you like it?"

Come into the water. It's the only place you'll believe me.

In Which She Is an Angry Dyke

"For a lesbian, you write an awful lot about men," said a man who was giving me more material. To live your entire life in a box just to be reminded of your own confines, as if you are not constantly destroying the box just to nail it back together.

Inversely, he asks, "What are your thoughts on men who write about lesbians?" Do you mean, what if you, as the first builder of the box, wrote of my experience in the very box you put me in? Does the wolverine write of the feline?

Of course it does.

But we've had to pull ourselves up by our boots, our long silver chains, to be noticed enough to get a seat at the table. Let me flip my box over as to sit on top of it, so we can be eye-level when I tell you to go fuck yourself. You will then tell me I am abrasive, outspoken, a bit too much, don't you think? And from my box I will pull out my history book of all the times you have directly and indirectly denounced my very existence, objectified me, caused me harm. I will show you keys between knuckles. You will be astounded to find what I can turn into a weapon.

I've never liked tattoos on women, never have. I just don't find them attractive.

You're going to eat all of that?

I love intelligent women.

You just haven't had the right dick before.

You can't break up with me. You need me.

You're too pretty to be gay.

What she meant to say was, _____.

Or what about the silent times? The "accidental slips" on the subway as your palm caresses my ass, followed by your, "God Bless." Where do you go to church? Throw your god away; skin yourself alive like you do to me when you listen to the higher power ingrained in you that tells you I am for you. When you have rid yourself of your belief that I grew from the sidewalk this morning just to be held in your gaze, then you will perhaps begin to read about women, about lesbians.

The wolverine that writes about women is the same wolverine that preaches illiteracy. So it's quite alright if you find me hard to swallow

    so are you from what I remember,

If you find me to be a little too much.

If you find that you'd like me better if I whispered to the walls in the Room of My Own. If you find me to be a rather loud, abrasive, opinionated, well-taught, well-read, bold lesbian who writes an awful lot about men.

Thank you and fuck you.

In Which She is Banned From Eternal Grace (and Grateful)

Thank ____. It isn't God. Although, this is the stuff of myths.

I am grateful for the things I thought were right but weren't. The sweet taste of what is incorrect, how we drink it in plentiful amounts.

In the way fluorescence makes the body transparent, a bathroom bar hookup is an honest adventure. The door being a portal to forgetfulness.

"Please don't look at me." But really, what else is there when you're looking anywhere else. When the point is to distract. Fill me so that I need not fill myself. This is a century old fable.

The kitchen: inherent confines. I followed recipes like scripture, setting an empty table, with hopes that flavor might seduce you. Usefulness makes a liar out of lovers.

What if we forgot our upbringings.

Declare yourself, so that we might become babes, lapping up milk beneath you, a rejuvenated species.

The tool that would build you a mountain to scream from would be a time machine.

I wish to be your salvation.

This country was built in a blood bath. Half of us have

been banned from eternal grace. But there is heaven in our loving one another. Identity is given, while hatred is learned. Let that take up a pew.

In church, men would shake the hands of married women and spend the rest of the gospel staring at their asses. Then, they'd tell me I was pretty, and therefore, they'd tell me I was worthy.

They must have been lonely, these unsaveable men.

The priest swayed up and down the aisles, hands peeking through too-large sleeves. Love is between a man and a woman, and I wait for the punchline.

Now my church is in the pockets of your laughter in bed in the morning. Shadow puppets on walls, we attempt to give our youth back to each other.

I still have to remind myself every day that my worth is not based on my willingness to get on my knees. I spent years there. To stand is to be liberated. When you find me on my knees, you must find yourself grateful. And I will wait while you pray.

I tried to fill my hands with skin and when I looked down, the boundaries of my own self were unrecognizable. In feigning affections for other people, we are able to lie to ourselves. I was an exhibition seen by everyone but myself. I suppose this is still art.

Now I come home to soft skin and sweet smiles, a story inked on a back.

I once told you that I would never write about you, about my love for you, because I wrote only of tragedy, calamity, destruction. This remains true, but in you, I write the inverse of that, the sweet sigh of the earth thanking us for settling in this moment.

It is sweeter than honey mixed in the tea I do not drink. Thank _____. Or whoever you scream for in bed.

In Which She Lives a Fairytale

Two women were born from the dirt of different lands. When they were strong enough to walk, they severed their roots and took off into the world. But they were not properly prepared for the bleakness, the depravity. The shadows spoke, foreboding a lifetime of trauma, recounting a history of pain. Eventually, the two women stumbled upon each other. Their pasts were too dissimilar, their pain too dichotomous. But still, they took each other as lovers.

Each woman dismissed the idea of happily ever after, invoking stories of ancestral void. But unspoken are many of our hopes. Laced in much of what we denounce is what we pray for at night.

One of them took paint to all the clocks in their house. For sheets could fall down too easily. This one believed that time was not linear. She believed that the Universe was a continuous loop, making it so that love never needed to exist in confines, for they could love again if the stars aligned once more. The other had not considered such things because the formula in her mind was set mostly to self-hatred, unable she was to envision tomorrow. But she hoped, prayed even, that they'd be together then.

They tried to heal one another tirelessly. But it was fruitless work. This they should have known. For no matter how many times the she-wolf licked her kin, Rome was still founded in violence.

One day, one of the women took all the clocks from the wall. Saying, if we stop keeping relics to measure time, then we can love one another in perpetuity, and then after, perhaps. But the other had stopped measuring time long before that. Allow me to love you without considering time at all—the lack of time. Allow for me to love you just right now, however long that is.

Eventually, love hangs weightlessly in the air, eclipsing all words. Memories are latent. Silence sits at the intersection of peace and violence.

Once upon a time, two women put the clocks in the rivers from where they're both from. And in climbing in after them, declared they were grateful to have shared anything at all.

In Which She Cries at a Wedding

When I first came out, I didn't know how to touch a woman. I figured out how to make myself cum when I was eleven, rubbing myself along the foot of my bed. I was embarrassed the day it was thrown away, my father and mother holding either side of it as they took the bed's pieces to the curb. Did they know? Could they smell my promiscuity like disease? They had signed divorce papers recently. I wondered if anyone ever took the bed or if it was recycled, upholstered, turned into a chair. I hope people love it.

I find eye contact harder when I'm certain I will lose more than my concentration in staring. I'm finding it difficult to remind myself things are worth the risk. "You'll never know until you try," they say, when sometimes knowing is the trouble.

I once dated a girl I could never have. That was my first mistake, confusing love for possession, confusing love for anything at all. I stared at her with a ferocity that said:

Please love me so that my queerness might be written in stone.

How naive, to think this would be easy, that I'd walk out of the closet and find the right person in urgency. Another concoction, another spoon under the pillow.

We forget that we can break our own hearts. We act violently against ourselves in cycles and seemingly unbreakable patterns. But in ruins, we become creatures of divine journey. We meet ourselves. I found I was not ready, to meet this version of myself. And so I let her take me to bed so many times, I moaned her name long after she was gone. For many months I could still taste her on my chin when I went to tongue food that missed my mouth. What is justice but just another foreign concept.

She would throw me around her room, slam me into walls, bend me over the dresser. To be objectified in the false safety of a home. I liked it this way, to be soulless, a body floating through a room. I had allowed men to handle me the same way. Swiftness allows for few thoughts to permeate one's mind. Was it Newton that said an object in motion stays in motion? What of the body and mind? When it comes to rest, it meets itself. There is no science in this.

We can spend most of our lives shoving square pegs in round holes if we decide we have affections for things that do not fit. We spend our youth playing make believe. Many of us forget to stop.

I once watched a couple dance at a wedding. They had been married 56-years. I wanted so badly to believe in the sanctity of anything.

In Which She Takes Multiple Lovers

There's a backyard in Brooklyn where I fell in love with multiple people at once.

Hair long or buzzed or half-and-half, dyed colors made in bowls in bathrooms with each other's fingers. We entered this life half-forgotten, scraps left atop a too-high counter. We were taught love in morse code. But we chose each other.

We kiss on the mouth.

We satiate every need.

I want to talk to you about prayer, about Sunday morning in Brooklyn. My place of worship is where I ground myself between them, beneath them. Digging my feet into the mattress the same way I would dirt.

I'm talking about the growth properties of dirt. The new beginnings. I'm not talking about needing a shower because we don't.

I want to stay here, become covered and uncovered and lose myself in animalistic tendencies. I want to taste yesterday.

The way we breathe, the way we forget to — it says everything.

I find difficulty in opening pickle jars and asking for what I need. They can smell my fear and leave the door unlocked for me.

This doesn't work if you don't.

At 20, I was dating the Founding Father of a fraternity. Boat shoes and pastels and hiding from myself.

I wanted so badly to be someone I was not.

At 21, I was dating a tall, lanky woman with long blonde hair who loved wine and hated the part of herself that wanted to fuck me. I tried to teach her love, but it was like speaking in tongues.

I wanted so badly to be someone I was not.

On Sunday mornings in Brooklyn, I wake up grateful. The dog's snout is pressed against my chin, and I can hear my partner's labored breathing. Even sleep takes work. It's all taken work — becoming these versions of ourselves where we pick out rugs and furniture and say I'm scared and I love you and I'd like for both to be okay.

What is intimacy without honesty? Lust.

We will survive the apocalypse, an ostracized class made bronze by deceit and violence. We will recite prayers from rooftops.

I am gay first and human second, or human first and gay second, or I am just a gay human and neither is first or second --

as in we are not second class citizens,

as in it's taken me a second to get here;

as in one more second in bed with them,

as in, first, let me finish;

as in I am first deep without the R (and grateful).

As in, first friends, lovers second or lovers first and friends second or
> at first we can't tell and now it doesn't matter.

As in, first, I want to bleed truth; I want to eat it the same way I do their spit (seconds, please),

as in, for the first time,

I want so badly to be no one else, a prayer recited in Brooklyn.

In Which She Eats Dirt

I feel I have learned so much without my permission.

You are sacred ground, the dirt of which I want to eat.

You love me for wanting to explore cemeteries, but I find it safe there. The dead must be the most sorry of us all.

I want to love you properly, so afraid I am of someone having loved you better. There is selfishness even *(especially)* in this.

How many moments I have ruined in the spaces between seconds.

Please whisper to me in the dark and tell me that there is no one like me. I am so sorry that I think the world owes me something, when I owe it everything—when it owes me nothing.

I look at you and see a summer lake, toes dipping in below a poignantly murky surface.

I have always been a decent swimmer.

You are a veranda porch and jazz music, lemonade at the ready. You make me have a craving for marmalade and honey, for a time I was not present for.

What is nostalgia but just an idea.

My mother begs me to be grateful for feeling so

much, but sometimes I feel like it must be a curse, a mark from Lucifer for not having joined him at birth.

I want to feel the wind on my back.

I am animalistic and also most human in the moments when we root ourselves into one another.

I remind you I love you so often because I am afraid the atmosphere has eaten my words. If I cannot hold you properly then I can at least lace your shoes up with my affections.

But who decided which way we were meant to love one another, and is it perhaps that I was trying too hard at all the wrong things.

I forget, sometimes, that love cannot be put in a jar the same way moisture pools between my legs.

I have only ever been one thing.

I think candles are so beautiful. The way they can light a room, or burn down a building.

I am grateful for just right now, the pockets of immediacy beneath our tongues.

I love you because language fails me. But it is so much more than that.

I sit between fearing I am too much, and fearing I am not enough.

I have only ever been two things.

Did I mention the rocking chair on the porch, the one down by the lake. Time ticks slowly on a clock that is not wound. I will still ask you again and again for the time.

Who am I in the pockets in between?

The summer stands still on the horizon. I feel how sticky I am, standing barefoot in the mud. Peach juice drips down my chin as I stare at a shadow moving toward me from the setting sun, muddling over words in my head for feelings much greater than language can muster. *I love you. I want all of it, the good, the bad, the ugly. Come to me on the darkest night and sit. Let me fill each tear with laughter—I have only just now remembered I am funny.* This shadow is moving closer, my knees sticky from the eagerness of fruit.

My heart beat drowns out the ticking of the clock.

I could remain here, waiting, forever.

In Which Language is of No Use

Flesh and skin are both tangible and elusive. I want to understand the earnestness of your desire, the archaic purity in your grasp, only by the taste of your spit.

Is this how you want me to fuck you?

Yes, this is how I want to make love.

There is such beauty in being corrected this way.

And again, language escapes me. Because every time I look at you I am making love to you.

I want to sit at the bottom of the pool with you. I want to, ever so briefly, quiet your mind. Therein lies a labyrinth of gossamer for which I have no map.

I believe I must have known you when we were dirt.

In choosing the physicality of things—in taking you in my mouth—I have shown you love in fractions.

The back of my throat yearns for the taste.

But more than that, I am afraid of the overflow of speech. That before long, poetry will cover the walls, and I will be standing before you in a foot of water, shedding skin.

Intimacy lies dormant in language.

I want to ask for your forgiveness, but it could quickly

turn to begging. Years after I denounced God, I find my hands folded. Perhaps I am praying to you. I have long said that God is other people.

What I know is simple: I love you in a way that is holy, pure in its animalistic tendency to over indulge. I am passing around the basket so that I may build a temple in which to dwell with you. But at my core, I know the emptiness in these gestures. The Dreamer seldom acts. Instead, her locked drawer is filled with blueprints, indecipherable — even to her.

In Which She Denounces Love

I heard a fairytale once, where they ended up together, where they lived happily ever after. And then I spent my whole life avoiding it, out of fear (knowledge) that they had gotten it all wrong. What if love is just a thing we do for a little while until we forget ourselves, pick up our backpacks and walk out into the cul-de-sac, frantic for any sign telling us where we are.

I think half of us are playing house with one another, picking out drapes and cutlery we will later use in violence when we realize we weren't saying what we meant. Life is a series of forgotten intentions and mislead people. But at our core, we are hopeful, and sometimes it is at the expense of being thoughtful.

It is exhausting to start and begin again in such excess. Each time, we hope, just this once. Sometimes we get it right, even in brevity. That's the crux of it, we forget to give validity to what does not last forever. Love need not be quantified by time, as though you have not once heard of an unhappy marriage. How respectable, two people who walk away when it's time and still remember when they loved each other and meant it.

I spent my teenage years being afraid of my father's heartbreak. Until one day when his anger finally resulted in tears, uninhibited sobs, his body shook. I changed my shoes that day. And swore I would never get close enough to suffer at the expense of a closing door.

It will take me years to realize that I am running from myself.

The mortgage, the white-picket fence, the two car garage, the things of 20th Century fairytales—I distaste their permanence. By which I mean, I want in excess for someone to be so certain of me, so certain of anything. By which I mean I hate that we have quantified love with possessions and paperwork, things such as long periods of time and basement safes.

It will take me years to realize that I am running from everything, from anything at all.

On Sadness, Pain, and Rebirth

I want to tell you a story of a phoenix born from ashes. But that is a story told in excess, a hat worn many times. In fact, it's much more simple than that: I felt pain; I suffered, and thus, I was reborn.

In Which She Writes in Red

I want for my skin to be on fire.

My mother washed plates with hot water, announcing that cold water was refreshing but not cleansing. Might I be reborn in the kitchen sink?

This skin is insufficient. How many lovers have taken me in their mouths just to later turn their faces up in disgust? At what point do we decide we are not a required taste, but indigestible entirely.

No one touches me like you do.
No one's ever made me cry from an orgasm.
You made me come alive.

We can speak poetry down each other's throats until our bellies are full, but eventually silence will glare back at us in bed. We pray for forever until forever becomes disease-like, an intruder in our home.

Timing is everything.

But how many of us are early, late, or just on time for the wrong people. What pain there is in being certain and incorrect.

Have we considered that the White Rabbit had a broken pocket watch?

I have never been a perfect lover.

I keep pickles, beer, and water in the fridge. I am ready for the divorce.

How much water has been wasted while I attempt to categorize illness. I write poetry in the shower in red, making it so that once a month, I cannot tell the ink from my blood.

A lover once made me scrub the mattress clean. Bleach and hot water, she said. I cleaned as I howled at the moon.

I wanted for her to drink my bath water. For her to house me like fine china. But instead, I was forced to tally the ways in which I made her sick.

That summer, the boiler in her house broke. I had been trying to wash it off in the shower: Myself. Everything.

In Which She Has a Visitor

I sleep with a hammer next to my bed because I have weaponized everything, even rest. In fits of tossing and turning, I smash holes into the walls and allow myself to stare at the intersection of destruction and beauty as the sun pours onto my naked body.

The morning forgives everything except me.

I have a fantasy of waking up in a house on the water. I'm still in this body because that is the part I have forgiven.

Even sometimes this is a lie.

The house has no roof, and I am allowed no weapons. Every morning a beautiful woman comes in and sits on the end of my bed. She stares at me, undresses herself. She reaches between her legs and sounds just like the ocean, smiling at me as her long hair falls around her face.

I am weakness.

I extend every inch of myself to try and please her, but she bounds me to the bed without so much as raising a spare finger. To be held in her gaze is to become motionless, a willing prisoner in my own bed.

This is my pleasure, her ocean tells me. You have not created this.

At the peak of climax, she opens her mouth in

ecstasy, and moths flood the room. I am released then from the bed, but as I reach to grasp her, she turns to vapor in my hands. I am covered in moths, and in spite of myself, can feel the ocean between my legs.

What if I forgave myself?

I spin in circles now, but nursery rhymes don't play in my head. I am still plagued by escapism, even in this house on the water. You mean to tell me that I can easily slip through the ceiling, watch the sun rise above the horizon, and slide out into the night, evading the woman at the end of my bed. But I am covered in moth dust, and they are the one things I will not smash with my hammer, and I am addicted to her ecstasy because I am relieved I did not create it because I am relieved I cannot fail her. And I am sickened to tell you that when it's just the moths and I, I grasp at the sheets where she sat, trying to taste what she's left behind, but all I can hear is the ever-present buzzing of insects on lights and the remnants of her at the end of the bed. But if I did not create her ocean, have I even existed in this moment with her? Could I be anyone? Am I anyone?

What if I forgave myself?

In Which She Reads the Prophecy

My mother once met a woman who refused to call herself a Witch.

This woman told my mother that she and I had traveled through many lives together—

that once I was a man;

that once I was Egyptian royalty.

That once people listened to me more concretely on account of my gender and class.

I didn't inherit my mother's love for crystals, her ability to meditate every morning. I do believe that Newton was right, that energy is neither created nor destroyed, yet I do not think he understood the broadness of his speech—that I would use his scientific theory to explain reincarnation—but men rarely do.

Since humanity has made itself clear about misunderstanding each other for centuries, we are forced to consider that Sartre was right, that hell really is other people.

>   In shooting each other,
>   in setting fire to trees,
>   in ensuring that Big Oil has
>   more ground to stand on than
>   Indigenous communities,
>   in incarcerating Black men with
>   more ferocity than we consider

>   funding disenfranchised
>   communities,
>   in doing things like
>   opening a fucking museum
>   for selfies in a city with a
> homeless population that
> could arm itself and revolt—
> we have proven that we have
>   forgotten each other entirely, that we
> are living in a Groundhog's Day-like
>   existence of learning, relearning, and
> forgetting.

But surely, hell cannot always be other people—not in the moments when my laughter pools in my stomach and aches, or when people are so honest that it overflows from them like a soda machine pressed too hard and forgotten about —

I want you to feel like you're on fire. I want you to understand the urgency there is in needing to advocate for your own life. It is unsurmountable when you feel you stand alone.

I have missed many of you before we've even met; my soul instantly knows you were missing from it for so long. There's people in my life with whom I have traveled under many moons. It is instantaneous, this love, beyond which is a force of nature so undeniable I must check that my feet are still on the ground.

So many of us have been loving each other under different names for centuries.

This woman who refused to call herself a Witch said

that so many of us come so close to changing everything, but so afraid we are of falling short that we become self-fulfilling prophecies, holding the fate of the world in hands we tried to stretch and never tried to fill.

"How do you know these things," I asked. "If you are not a witch?"

"Because each morning the birds regurgitate the world onto my front porch."

I realized that I am too young for so much and too old for everything else.

In Which She Makes the Bed

I've come to realize that

> I don't know how to do

>> any of this.

I have always been told that I am too much, or not enough, and so...

I become small, or large, or just the right size for nothing at all.

I wanted so badly to be stuck between her teeth.

I want to be your greatest love of all, but fear sits on my chest like bricks. I have read many epics on love. But when does the chaise lounge become the world? How valiant it is to embark.

Will I live to see the other side? Will I succeed? Will you dream of me even while I'm lying next to you? Will there always be desperation in the way you wait for me to finish a task? Please remember me at my best. Please love me at my worst.

I want to feel the wind on my back.

I am so scared of being wrong, of being only pretty.

Can the dog smell my illness?

Loving you is relearning everything I've ever known, but it's no use. For the dog can surely smell my illness. And no matter how many times I fluff the pillows or fold the top sheet down, I am reminded they are not my pillows, it is not my sheet, it is not my bed.

I ask you to lobotomize me. You take me in your arms and kiss my eyelids, but I swore I would not cry.
You tell me you love me in a foreign tongue.

I am counting what does not belong to me.

In Which She Draws a Bath for Grief

Grief comes and sits next to me, pats my hand, and says, "We've done this many times, you and I." She's in gossamer and lace, and ever-so-briefly I am convinced she is here for me.

"That would be too easy," she says. And of course, she is right.

She does not visit only in death, for we suffer loss at much less. And no matter how much I have grown used to her, all air leaves my lungs at the sight of her. Who am I without her? After the first visit, we never know.

In these moments, we find out who we are without other people. And it's always the answer we feared.

She draws me a bath, stirs in bubbles and then removes them, lights the candles and blows them out. She drinks the bath water and when she is satiated, motions for me to climb in. There is certainty in every void.

She does not trust me not to drown.

We sit together and talk in silence. It is powerful, what we need not say. Grief is second nature, an aspect of evolution in a world fixated on self-destruction.

I write her letters when she is gone. I am indebted to her sadness. There is seldom poetry without it.

I allow for the paper to dissolve in the water. The words are etched onto my skin, prayer cards and apologies and things not said.

There is so much hesitancy in life.

So much regret in death.

In Which the Ocean is Made of Tea

I used to distaste the ocean. People would cite the calm inherit in the waves, the cleansing properties of salt. I just saw another thing that could disappoint me.

My mother used to make me tea to cure everything. Yet I remain sick. If I trace the origins of all of my thoughts, I will find that insanity is genetic.

Now, the ocean mist masks tears of lovers and my own. On the shore, with the sun cascading below the horizon and the birds chirping—the lines where we begin and end are blurred. I have longed for this sense of confusion. For the passion that ensues when you are enthralled with the lack of boundaries associated with love. I have no borders here.

There is something indescribable about life: at first. The first kiss, the first time you allow the ocean to hit your toes, the way her smile hits you in waves and then blankets you in unchartered intimacy. It is unfathomable that you ever left the beach, that life started without your permission. I am sand in an hourglass. And I still denounce the shape.

Cliffs are good for falling off of, but mostly for screaming off the edge of. What would happen if we screamed in earnest on the subway, on the street, in a crowd? How unfathomable, to not unleash our anger at the ends of the earth.

If I close my eyes, I am in the ocean. The waves and I taunt each other, a playful ecstasy. I take salt water in my mouth and gargle. I want to drown, but I do not wish to die.

The kettle rings in the kitchen.

I hear my mother calling.

In Which She Realizes She is Miserable

The taste in my mouth is reminiscent of many bitten tongues.

How many martyrs were created before the mirror was finally made sacrilegious.

Unworthiness is hereditary. But I have never been good with a needle and thread.

Every night the walls peel back because I beg for them to.

I am afraid I may die saying, *Please* or *I'm sorry.*

I count the pennies to keep my mind busy.

My father points to the planes, and I imagine I am one.

I want to stop asking if you love me. But I think I am waiting to be right.

An ancestor of mine once bit her own tongue off, drowned in her own blood. I admire her tenacity.

In Which She Picks Up Botany

Soft coffee promises in the morning, your hand lingers until it becomes phantom-like in mine.

My bed is a cemetery, and I can recite the names, but I do not wish to become a deterrent before we even start.

The flowers next to my bed are dead, but it is not for a lack of trying. They need water, not compassion, and only one flows from my fingers.

Spit profanity and love into my mouth, and we can play a game of which is which.

I have never known anyone. Life is a box of forgotten-about things under my bed that I refuse to let go of just in case they come back to me, but like the flowers, they are dead, and like the dust, I never learn my lesson.

When does a pattern become a lifestyle choice?

I've been tired a long while now, addicted to other people's Valium and the sound of laughter. I will lick every last drop off your tongue before I even think to tell you I am drowning.

And I still won't.

Give me your vulnerable. Give me your intimate. Give me the broken down masses, the philosophical for the sake of the argument. The deep questions at midnight because we hope with desperation to be seen from answering to our biggest fears. Give me your weak and your tired helpers. Give me those that overflow until there is nothing else left. Give me the women who leak like rivers when connection strikes just to drown themselves in their own joy.

Watch as we dig our fingers into our emptinesses as to create more space for what is not ours. Because even the painful is better than the hollow.

In this, we become blind.

The vines are visible, growing tendrils up my spine.

We shout accusations until we realize we are screaming at ourselves. The mirror is also an abyss. One hangs at the end of my bed.

In Which She is Nothing (And Therefore, Something)

I am writing the grocery list
Like poetry.

There is no time anymore.

I want to unzip my skin, shed, step out into the center of the room, open the windows and beg in earnest. For the sun. The stars. For anything other than copper on my tongue.

I sometimes confuse afterbirth and rebirth. But it is only the latter I am after.

I want to be touched in a way that results in crumbled paper on the floor. Indescribable, but not with a lack of trying.

Children will be forced to read history books upside down, backwards. In this, they will hope for answers.

If I become a snake to shed my skin, then perhaps I will be reborn. Yet my allegiances are not with the connotation of a snake. I do not want my character confused.

I have taken up running with the hopes that the next outdoor adventure will result in wings. But I do not wish to be a bird.

The days in which I feel remarkably ordinary are of most importance.

I once sat on the edge of the Grand Canyon and told the space next to me that I was insignificant. It was liberating.

To be nothing.

Acknowledgements

Thank you to my family - my mother and father especially, who have supported every change of heart, every endeavor; without you I wouldn't be who I am today. I wish we lived in a world where I need not be grateful for your acceptance of me, but alas, here we are. Thank you for never making me explain, for working to create a world of wholeness and love for all queer children.

To my friends - my queer, chosen family - you breathe a life force into me that allows for art like this. To know you is to love you. To know you has been to love myself.

To my partner, Cass, who has known exactly when to close that study door, who took the photograph that is now the cover of this very book, and who holds space for me that is gentle, kind, and filled with love. To journey with you through this life is one of many pleasures.

And to every lover, especially the ones who have caused me pain, thank you. Without pain, there is seldom art. To the ones who I have hurt, thank you for sharing a part of your life with me; I'm sorry I took it for granted.

Thank you for reading.

All my love.

www.ingramcontent.com/pod-product-compliance
Lightning Source LLC
Chambersburg PA
CBHW021451070526
44577CB00002B/361